CARS IN CUBA
YOU SHOULD SEE BEFORE THEY DIE

Photographs and words by

KIM BUDDEE

NEW HOLLAND

CONTENTS

FOR CINDY

PREFACE

About four years ago I created a picture book about Burma. It was inspired by the imminent prospect of this hermit country coming out of mothballs and joining the 21st century. I set about recording aspects of the culture and environment that I thought would be changed, or lost forever, by the onset of this 'Burmese spring'. Upon publication, people commonly asked about my next project and helpfully suggested that perhaps when Fidel Castro died, I should gather images of Cuba before it was engaged in a similar transformation. As it happened, history took its own course and in December 2014, US President Obama began a process of re-engagement and detente with Cuba. Even without the demise of *El Jefe* I could see pretty soon, that things would start to change so I put the wheels in motion to take a portrait of the country on the cusp of a new era.

Further developments in 2015, resulted in embassies being re-established in the respective countries and in March 2016, a US President visited Cuba for the first time in eighty years. Finally, in December of that same year, Fidel Castro passed away. Cuba would never be the same again.

While taking a broad and open-minded approach to all things Cuban, in spite of myself, I was captivated by the bulky yet magnificent 'yank tanks' I encountered growling and prowling Cuba's roads. I came across well-known brands such as Ford and Chevrolet and discovered forgotten marques including Desoto, Studebaker and Nash. As a baby boomer these zombies from the 1940s and 50s piqued childhood memories. As luck would have it, not only was our family car a green 1953 Ford Customline but my own first car was an FJ Holden. Everywhere I turned in the time-warp cities, towns and country, my pictures seemed incomplete without the inclusion of one of these beautiful beasts that together had turned Cuba into a kind of Jurassic Park of motor vehicles. The collection of snap shots presented here, is my tribute to these *cacharros*, long may they reign.

INTRODUCTION

Cuba was one of the greatest importers of American cars in the first half of the 20th Century and by 1955 they numbered over one hundred and fifty-five thousand. In January 1959, Fidel Castro's victorious revolutionary army took control of Cuba. Over the next eighteen months, his government's actions would see an end to the fabulous era of American cars.

In the following years, Soviet automobiles especially Ladas and Vaz were imported together with smaller numbers of European models. More recently Asian imports — especially Chinese — are altering the motor landscape, yet it's estimated that over sixty thousand pre-1960 American cars continue to operate on the roads of Cuba. They survive thanks to the ingenuity and persistence of their Cuban owners and also due to the original engineering excellence of these sturdy motor vehicles from Detroit, Michigan.

These days, the 1950s American car as a Cuban icon is changing. In December 2013, the Castro regime lifted the half-century ban on the importation of foreign cars to Cuba and their purchase without government approval. This decision is bringing an end to the numerical dominance of old cars on the island's streets — especially the classic American variety. Better public transport options are also diminishing the importance of these worn out cars as an integral component of Cuba's transport. In time, many or perhaps all of the ancient cars will be renovated and restored to their glamorous former glory and eventually become the expensive and exclusive province of cashed up tourists leaving the unvarnished hybrid mashed up original jalopies seen on the streets of today, to fade away, like those ubiquitous posters of Fidel and Che.

ON THE STREETS

Stepping out of your hotel and wandering the dusty streets lined with shabby Spanish colonial buildings, you could easily believe yourself in some down at heel town in Spain or a struggling part of South or Central America. The crude mural depicting Che Guevara may give you a clue but, as soon as a 1950s Chevrolet rattles past followed by a Buick or Ford or Oldsmobile, you know for sure that you're in Cuba.

You stand near the corner of Calle Neptuno and El Prado in Central Havana, next to the fruit market. There will be a handful of Cubans waiting too. A *maquina* (slang for car) will turn up in no time and when you or someone else raises their hand, it may stop if there's a spare seat. After some negotiation over the price and depending where you are on the pecking order, you may be forced to sit in the front middle seat. Then, off you go and if your Spanish is good enough, you can have a robust conversation with the driver and other customers sharing the ride. From time to time the old bone-shaker will stop and people will get off and others will get in and you may gradually shuffle away from the front seat to the side or rear.

These shared taxis known as *colectivos* often run on fixed, long-distance routes, for example, from central Havana to the western suburbs of Miramar or Marianao via the Malecón. They also favour the famous Calle 23 known as *La Rampa*. Now and then a Russian Lada taxi may pass, yet over ninety per cent of the vehicles are the spacious American models. These aren't the glossy glamorous convertibles seen touting for customers beside the tourist hotels, but bog-standard, hand-painted, rusty, clunky rigs blasting out diesel fumes, more akin in style to Mad Max than Mad Men.

Cuban streets function as the people's living rooms, playgrounds, garages and workshops. A 1953 Chevrolet awaits treatment in Regla, an unvarnished sleepy suburb across the harbour from Havana.

OPPOSITE – In front of Havana's beautiful Gran Teatro, restored Buick, Chevrolet, Oldsmobile, Pontiac, Mercury and Ford convertibles line-up for their opportunity to take tourists on sightseeing spins around Havana.

A 1952 Chevrolet is parked outside Dos Hermanos, a harbour-side bar that has been in operation since 1905. This drinking spot became especially popular in the 1920s as first port of call for American tourists temporarily escaping their Prohibition era abstinence.

OPPOSITE – A 1955 Oldsmobile outside the Floridita bar, renowned as the 'cradle of the *daiquiri*', a cocktail reputedly originating in the eastern town of Daiquiri. Constantino Ribalaigua, who presided over La Floridita for forty years, invented a grapefruit version called *Papa Dobles*, for his famous patron, Ernest Hemingway.

Calle Neptuno at night.

OPPOSITE – One of the oldest theatres in Havana is the Payret Cinema situated opposite the monumental Capitolio building which was once the Cuban seat of government.

A 1955 Chevrolet braves the downpour in Viñales.

OPPOSITE – On the edge of old Havana is the historic Iglesia Del Angel Custodio established in 1693. The green car is an early 1950s Dodge.

Taking a break on the Punta Gorda, Cienfuegos.

OPPOSITE – A Jeep on the road to Boca de Yumurí on Cuba's far east coast.

Locals take their time in the Baracoa morning to greet their neighbours and friends.

OPPOSITE – A glorious string of *carros* (cars) heads up Calle Neptuno west towards Vedado.

OLD TIMERS 1928-1942

You generally see vintage cars in motor museums, special Concors d'Elegance type events and motor shows but on this Caribbean island, a selection of these cars can be seen on the everyday streets pottering along as taxis or limo-style transport. The more you look, the more you realise that you can see and experience, the mid 20th century history of the American motor car being played out upon the streets of Cuba.

Cuba's love affair with the motor car started in 1898 with a French vehicle known as a 'Parisienne'. There were over 4,000 motorised vehicles in Havana by 1910. The first Chevrolet arrived in 1912 and a year later the first Ford. In 1918 they staged the first Interprovincial Road Race. The number of vehicles grew to 20,000 by 1920. Ready finance was making Cuba the number one automotive market in Latin America, with Cubans buying new cars faster than their neighbours in Argentina, Brazil and Mexico. The one thing stopping greater adoption of motor vehicles was the lack of roads, and it would take until 1931 for a sealed road to link the ends of the island.

The market continued to grow, bottomed out with the Wall Street crash of 1929 and then gradually picked up again in the 1930s. The battle between the car giants of GM and Ford was also played out on the Cuban streets and by the mid 30s these two manufacturers accounted for a third of the all the US made cars shipped to Cuba. In 1940, when Ford produced its 28 millionth car, bandleader Xavier Cugat was playing Perfidia and in that same year Colonel Batista won the Cuban presidential election. The new government put in place a remarkably progressive constitution that could have seen the country's history take a much different course had subsequent governments respected its integrity. This wasn't to be however, so the revolving door of presidents and/or dictators, civil unrest and American intervention in Cuba would continue.

When the US declared war on Japan, Germany and Italy in December 1941, Cuba followed suit. In 1942, all passenger car production ceased in the USA with the motor companies totally engaged in the war effort. For instance, Ford built over a quarter of a million Jeeps and over 8,000 B-24 Liberator bombers, Chevrolet built thousands of trucks, Buick made tank-destroyers and engines, Hudson made aircraft components and Studebaker made trucks and amphibious craft. Over the war years the number of cars in Cuba fell about twenty-five per cent, from 29,000 down to 22,000.

At the beginning of the 1930s cars stylistically appeared little changed from their predecessors from the 1920s, they still sported vertical rear ends, radiators and windscreens, separate headlights and unskirted fenders. Throughout the decade these attributes changed with radiators retreating behind stylish grilles and windscreens and rears sloping more elegantly. Fenders would start to skirt the wheels which were moving away from the wire style. Closer to the 1940s you saw running boards start to disappear and headlamps become integrated into the front fenders. The 'alligator hood' which opened at the front rather than sides meant shallower grilles. Radios, automatic wipers and heating and air-conditioning would start to appear although with automatic transmissions it would take the war years to iron out the wrinkles.

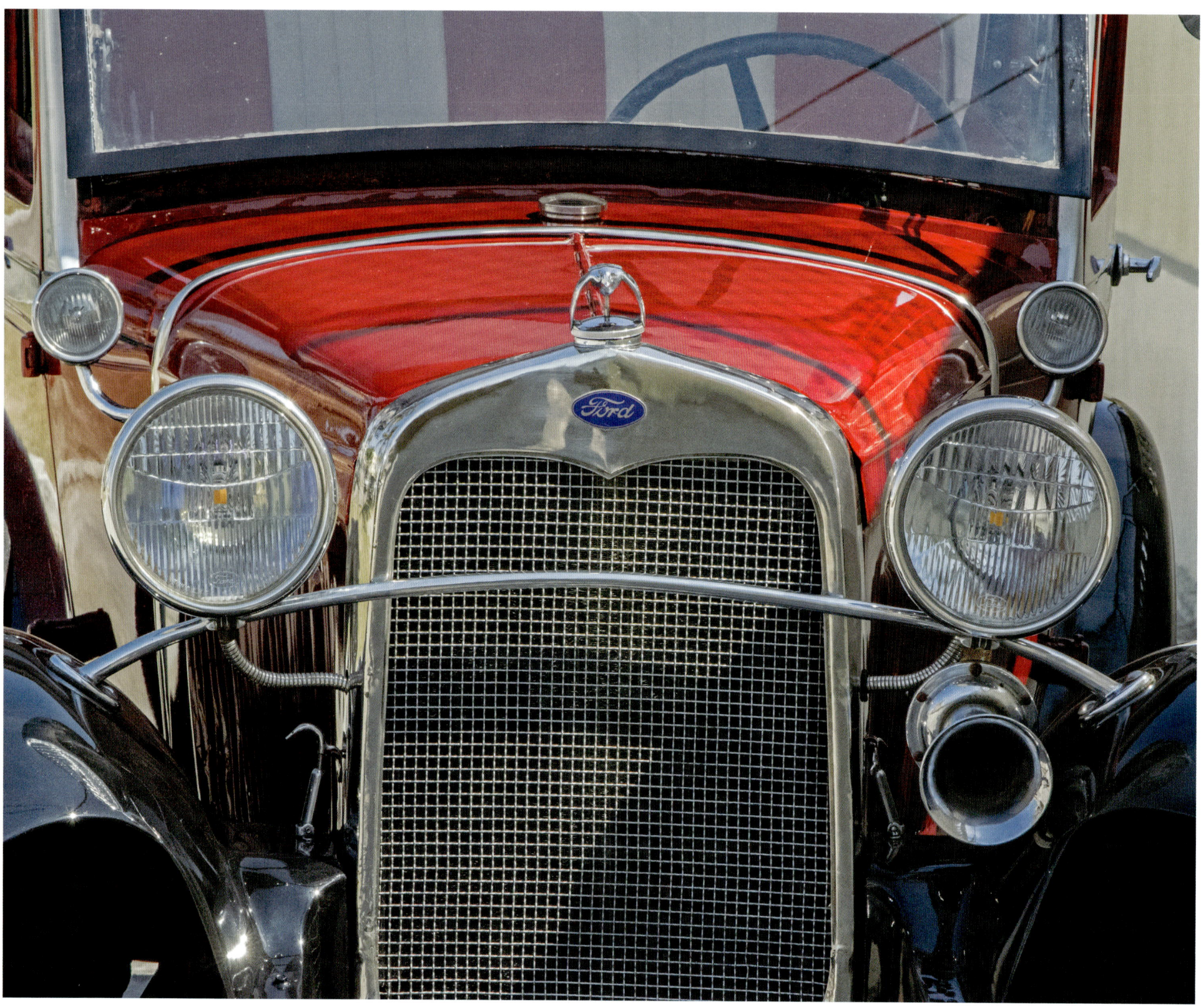

A 1928 Model A Tudor sedan. Henry Ford was reluctant to move on from the Model T and the company's fortunes waned until the launch of this new model which became Ford's next big success. It was manufactured from 1927 to 1932 and over 5 million were sold in that time.

OPPOSITE – The Ford Model A was born in 1928, the same year as Ernesto 'Che' Guevara, the Argentinian doctor who would go on to become a legend of the Cuban Revolution.

A 1937 Chevrolet that's lost its original grille and hood ornament, sports a front bumper that could have come from a Willys Jeep.

OPPOSITE – A convertible 1928 Ford Model A passes the Parque Centrale Hotel, Havana.

The rugged and famed American vehicle of the war years, the Willys Jeep, was also adopted by Castro's revolutionary forces in their struggle in the 1950s. It was in a Jeep that Castro made his victorious journey across Cuba from Santiago de Cuba to Havana, in January 1959. Castro was also quite partial to the English-made Land Rover, his bullet-marked vehicle can be seen at the Museo de la Revolución in Havana.

OPPOSITE – The 1938 Ford Deluxe Station Wagon—'designed for style as much as utility'. These models came to be known as 'woodies', with their ash trimmings and panels on the sides which were totally unsuited to Cuba's climate, requiring constant maintenance and revarnishing.

A 1941 Chevrolet Master Deluxe rumbles towards Havana's *Barrio Chino* (Chinatown).

OPPOSITE – A 1940 Ford which has a grille either salvaged from another car or hand made in a backyard workshop.

GUAGUAS E CAMIONES

When you encounter Cuba's walking dead of motor vehicles you can't ignore the unique and funky collection of larger vehicles. Many trucks do 'normal' service in Cuba, carrying produce and materials, but more often than not they are seen carrying people. In some cases you may find a simple tip-truck with passengers clinging to the hot metal sides whereas others have the rear section enclosed in a metal roof. There may be standing room only or some may have metal benches giving some semblance of comfort to the occupants. A number of these so called buses, known as *camiones*, have sliding glass windows and fully enclosed cabins but in essence are just old converted trucks. These often dangerously massive beasts are invariably crowded and steamy in the ever humid and hot climate.

This mishmash of vehicles forms a vital part of the transportation system of Cuba particularly since the fuel crisis of the 1990s Special Period and also because the rail network had been allowed to deteriorate. Some American-looking, second-hand, yellow school buses are actually from Canada and there are hand-me-down buses from Spain and Holland. Mercifully some newer buses are being imported from China and maybe in time the *camiones* may go back to being trucks. In the larger towns these local buses—known in the Cuban vernacular as *guaguas*—work fixed routes, to somewhat loose timetables They stop at *paradas*, the bus stops where an informal form of queuing operates. They will also pick up people along the main roads and highways, if there's room.

The driver cleans the windscreen of his 1950 Ford F6 truck as a 1958 Buick Special Riviera flashes past.

A 1950 International truck in front of Havana's Museo de la Revolución formerly the grandiose Presidential Palace. Behind is the SAU-100 tank used by Castro during the 1961 Battle of the Bay of Pigs.

OPPOSITE – A 1950 Dodge truck rigged as a bus, pulls away from the modest cafe situated near the Rio Arimao on the road from Playa Rancho Luna. It's displaying the destinations: Pasa Caballo and La Milpa in the Cienfuegos area.

On a hilly corner in Santiago de Cuba, the lack of
emission controls and old diesel engines produces
smoky streets and to make matters worse, most cars in
Cuba use leaded petrol which adds to the pollution. In
front is a 1953 Ford F600.

OPPOSITE – A truck passes along the wind swept
Malecón in Baracoa. The converted rear section
provides crude accommodation for passengers with
flaps to keep out the rain. The early 1950s Ford has
acquired quad headlights.

In the morning mist, a truck heads off towards the pass in the Sierra de los Órganos in western Cuba. These mountains are known for their dramatic karst outcrops known in Cuba as *mogotes*.

OPPOSITE   A bus traverses the rich farmland of the Viñales area in western Cuba.

An old truck is dwarfed by the grandiose monument to Che Guevara in Santa Clara.

The unrecognisable hulk of a truck resting on blocks, dominates a narrow street in Cienfuegos.

OPPOSITE – A 1955 Chevrolet has its rear tray converted for use as a small bus, servicing Cuba's north coast town of Caibarién.

BOTH – A Chevrolet removal truck
in La Habana Vieja.

In Baracoa, a 1957 Ford survives as a mini-bus.

OPPOSITE – A GMC school bus in Havana.

An ex-Canadian school bus (still displaying its school sign in French) in front of the outstanding art-deco building, once the biggest in Havana that was the headquarters of the Bacardi company known for its rum and other spirits. The family from Santiago de Cuba, were originally strong supporters of the Castro cause but after the revolution their assets were confiscated. They continued their business off-shore and were active opponents of the regime in the 1960s.

OPPOSITE – Despite the temperature and humidity there are no shortage of customers packing into this mini-bus in Santiago de Cuba.

A more luxurious 1960s Hino bus near Viñales.

OPPOSITE – A bulky 1951 Ford F1 pickup modified to carry passengers in Remedios.

POST WAR 1945-1949

The American car producers were sanctioned to get back into production in mid 1945. Many of the early models were re-hashes of pre-war models and it took a few years before new vehicles with fresher design elements were released. It would take Cadillac, Ford and Studebaker to introduce more modern styles away from the bulky beetle-like shapes of the 1940s. (There remained some resistance to lowering rooflines while men continued to wear hats, but fashions would change.)

The big three manufacturers at this time were Ford, General Motors and Chrysler. Ford would go on to make models under the Ford, Mercury, Lincoln and Edsel badges. General Motors had Cadillac, Chevrolet, Pontiac, Buick and Oldsmobile. Chrysler's marques included Desoto, Dodge and Plymouth. The independents were Studebaker, Kaiser-Frazer, Hudson, Packard, Willys and Crosley.

The diversity in car brands would continue to shrink. In 1929 the independent manufacturers accounted for twenty per cent of the market, by 1952 this would shrink to thirteen per cent and in a few years, just 4 per cent. By the time the Cuban revolution came in 1959 and US imports were halted, the remaining US companies were reduced to just GM, Ford, Chrysler, American Motors (Nash merged with Hudson) and Studebaker (merged with Packard).

Cuba mirrored America, and demand for vehicles ramped up after the war. The 16,258 cars registered in 1946 grew to 77,017 by 1952. The war's end would also see Cuba growing in popularity as an American tourist destination and set the scene for the boom times of the 1950s.

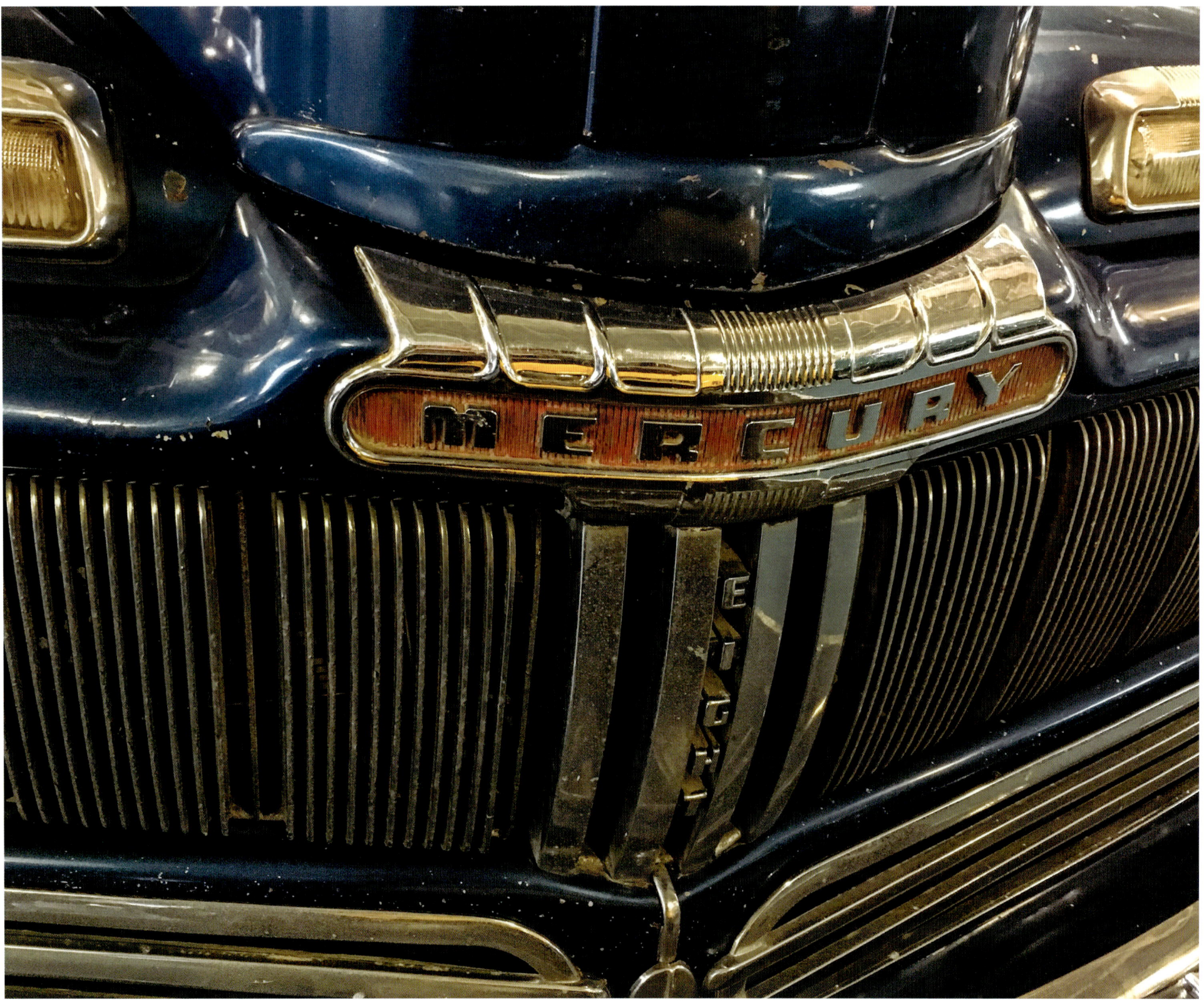

A 1946 Plymouth Deluxe in a side street of Cienfuegos. This car still incorporates 'suicide doors', the dangerous and infamous rear hinged forward opening rear doors, so useful to the Chicago gangsters in collecting and disposing of their passengers.

OPPOSITE – The intricately detailed front of a 1946 Mercury Eight. Ford's Mercury and Lincoln divisions re-commenced production in November 1945.

A 1946 Dodge opposite Havana's Museo Nacional de Bellas Artes de La Habana.

The 1946 Plymouth Deluxe is not so deluxe after seventy years.

OPPOSITE – A 1946 Ford Station Wagon used as a *colectivo* (taxi) in Baracoa in Cuba's east. A model that was marketed as: 'Smoother than ever-it's a new ride!'.

1947 Pontiac Streamliner with regular sedan body shape.

OPPOSITE – The 1947 Pontiac Streamliner Fastback. Castro's forces in the revolutionary war used a similar model that can be seen at the Granma Memorial in Havana.

1947 Chevrolet Fleetmaster.

OPPOSITE – 1947 Chevrolet
Fleetmaster with painted grille.

The 1947 Dodge Custom was little changed from its 1946 predecessor.

OPPOSITE – A gangster attending the infamous Mafia Summit in Havana in 1948 may have travelled in a 1948 Dodge Custom similar to this – although they probably chose a more prestigious and expensive Cadillac.

The 1948 Plymouth Deluxe brings a trailer of produce to the morning markets on the outskirts of Santa Clara.

OPPOSITE – 1948 Chevrolet Fleetmaster Grille.

A 1948 Chevrolet Fleetmaster with Havana's famous El Morro Castle beyond.

OPPOSITE – This crusty 1948 Plymouth is a work in progress.

The 1949 Plymouth hardly changed between 1945 and 1949.

OPPOSITE – 1948 Chevrolet Fleetmaster and 1949 Plymouth with non-standard grille.

EMBRACING THE AMERICAN DREAM 1950–1954

When you hear an American President talking about making his country great again then it's quite possible he's talking about the decade when he grew up. It's fair to say that in the 1950s America probably was the greatest country in the world. At the same time that the people in Asia, Africa and South America were struggling with poverty and throwing off the shackles of colonialism and while the Europeans were licking their wounds after the devastation of World War II, the American people enjoyed the highest standard of living in the world. A new era of consumerism and growth of families was embraced. People moved out to the new suburbs and filled their new houses with new refrigerators, washing machines and other goods still considered luxuries in the wider world. To access this new world were new highways, freeways, underpasses and overways and the motor cars reigned supreme as the mode of transport. It was the era of drive-in movies, drive-in hamburger joints, motels (motor-hotels), motor-homes and trailer parks.

The new models were large in size and driven by larger engines. They began to incorporate options unheard of in their counterparts in Britain, Europe and Japan like automatic transmissions, power steering, electric windows, air conditioning, push button radios and the powerful V8 engine which replaced the Straight 6. Competition was fierce among the manufacturers and styling became the point of difference to woo the buyers. Cars became lower and longer and new formats appeared such as the two-door hardtop and the station wagon. The 1950s became the golden age of the automobile.

Coincidentally the same period in Cuba was also a time of high hopes and prosperity. This small island neighbour of the rich United States was thriving more than anywhere else in Latin America. Not only were they reaping the benefits of their massive sugar exports but they also benefitted as the most popular holiday destination for everyday Americans. Although time stood still in rural areas, in the cities, esspecially with the growing middle class, Cubans embraced the American dream. They too built highways, high rise offices and flash hotels and constructed new spilt level homes with all the latest appliances installed. Above all they embraced the automobile.

And the automobile of choice was American. Ninety-five per cent of Cuba's cars came from Detroit and Cuba became the largest importer of US vehicles. There were more Cadillacs per capita than anywhere else in the world and in absolute terms, the number of motor vehicles in Cuba compared favourably with the larger countries of Argentina, Brazil and Mexico.

In 1949, Fulgencio Batista, who had left Cuba in 1944 after losing the election, returned, serving as a senator. He stood for President in the 1952 elections and fearing he would lose, staged a bloodless coup and became President. A young lawyer, Fidel Castro, stood for parliament in those elections and was understandably embittered by the outcome.

Frustrated by this illegitimate regime, Castro conceived a guerrilla attack on the Moncado Barracks in Santiago de Cuba. Financed by the sale of Abel Santamaria's Buick and the cashed-in pension plan of a Pontiac salesman called Jesus Montane, a force of 165 men was gathered for the assault. Castro's 1950 Chevrolet had broken down so he hired a 1952 Buick, Montane brought his 1959 Pontiac and Raúl Castro had a 1951 Chevrolet.

On July 26th 1953, with a fleet of 26 cars they set out against a force of about a thousand of Batista's soldiers. The daring action was a disaster with most assailants killed and the survivors including Castro and his brother Raúl, captured and sentenced to fifteen years in prison on the Island of Pines.

A 1950 Chevrolet, 1951 Chevrolet and 1952 Chevrolet in central Havana. It's no surprise Chevrolets were the best selling cars in Cuba at the time.

RIGHT – The 1950 Ford Custom carried forward the style elements of the innovative 1949 model with the slab-sided body shape and longer, lower styling that garnered it the Fashion Academy Award. Featuring the notable centre 'spinner' nose decoration, this model put Ford back in the big-time sales-wise. It was available with a straight 6 and V8 engine.

The 1950 Studebaker Champion with its jet-prow guided missile 'spinner' grill. These radically re-styled cars had short hoods and long trunks, hence their nickname 'coming or going Studebakers'. Their form came from the legendary studio of Raymond Loewy and outstanding designer Virgil Exner.

OPPOSITE – The tail of a 1950 Oldsmobile Futuramic 88 already shows a fin beginning to develop on its rear fender. It included a powerful Rocket V8 engine that overshadowed its stablemate GM's Cadillac at the time and gave it a top speed in excess of a 100 miles per hour. The car also inspired the 1951 song, ROCKET 88, by Jackie Brenston and his Delta Cats (led by Ike Turner), considered to be the first ever rock 'n' roll record.

A 1950 Series 62 Cadillac roars past the decrepit buildings on Havana's waterfront, sporting the baby fins inspired by the Lockheed P-38 fighter plane and first seen on the trail-blazing 1948 model.

OPPOSITE – A 1950 Chevrolet across from the Museo Historico de Guanabacoa.

The 1951 Ford was little changed from the 1950 model and was limited in production due to the Ford Motor Company's efforts towards the Korean War.

OPPOSITE – This 1951 Chevrolet came out in the same year as the all-time great American sitcom I LOVE LUCY debuted on television. Lucille Ball's on screen and real husband was Cuban actor and musician Desi Arnaz, who was already well known for his song, Babalú and several movies. In the show, he played a band leader at a club in New York, called the Tropicana.

This 1951 Chev appears to be welded to the street.

OPPOSITE – This 1951 Mercury Eight is little different from the 1949 model that was famously driven by James Dean in REBEL WITHOUT A CAUSE. Nearby, charging down Galiano is a 1955 Chevrolet and in the background is the notable art-nouveau facade of La Casa Quintana, once one of Havana's most prestigious places to shop.

A 1951 Pontiac huddles within a cluster of taxis outside the historic Hotel Inglaterra, open since 1875 and host to celebrities including ballerina Anna Pavlova and José Martí, the hero of Cuban independence.

A 1952 Buick Special De Luxe dominates a narrow street in La Habana Vieja, the oldest part of the city.

OPPOSITE – A 1952 Buick Special De Luxe cruises down Vedado's Calle 23. When this car was new, this wide sloping street known as La Rampa was a strip of seedy theatres, casinos and cabarets that epitomised the allure and attraction of mid-century Havana.

A 1952 Buick Roadmaster Riviera convertible with its distinctive Ventiports, three for the cheaper Buicks and four for the lavish Roadmaster.

OPPOSITE – This 1952 Chevrolet is undergoing some serious maintenance work in a Havana street.

The 1952 Chevrolet is parked in the Paseo de Marti, opposite the Capitolio Nacional with the immaculate Gran Teatro de La Habana in the background.

OPPOSITE – 1952 Chevrolet Styline Deluxe Station Wagon.

A 1952 Ford Customline taxi is tailed
by a 1948 Chevrolet Fleetmaster
through busy Centro Habana.

OPPOSITE – 1952 Chevrolet Styline
Deluxe Station Wagon.

A 1952 Ford Customline in a quiet side street in Trinidad, one of Cuba's oldest towns.

OPPOSITE – 1952 Mercury Monterey.

A 1952 Plymouth Cambridge in the rich farmland near Baracoa. The rear body has been converted into a cargo tray. This utility or 'ute' format with the cargo tray integrated into the car body was developed in Australia initially to suit the farmers wanting a vehicle for work and pleasure. Later Ford would reproduce this format with the popular Ranchero model and Chevrolet followed with its legendary El Camino.

OPPOSITE – This 1952 Plymouth Cranbrook looks right at home beside the genuine 1950s bar in Havana's Vedado area.

A stunning 1952 Pontiac Chieftain convertible parked outside the once glamorous shopping mall, the Manzana de Gómez, being rebirthed as a hotel.

OPPOSITE – A 1953 Buick Special shares a carpark with fleet of Cocotaxis, Havana's three wheel, three-seater, scooter-driven taxi.

A 1953 Mercury with modified front grille.

OPPOSITE – A 50th Anniversary 1953 Ford Customline overtakes a Chevrolet at Parque Centrale.

A 1953 Chevrolet with non-standard grille.

OPPOSITE – In Havana's Parque El Curita a 1953 Chevrolet overtakes a 1955 Plymouth Savoy. The '53 Chev was the first of the Bel Air models which went on to become one of Cuba's most popular cars.

1953 Pontiac Chieftain.

OPPOSITE – 1953 Dodge Coronet.

1953 Buick Super Riviera Coupe.

OPPOSITE – A 1953 Buick passes a 1955 Chevrolet and a local bus on the Carr Turística beside the Bahía de Santiago de Cuba.

A 1954 Plymouth Belvedere makes a pit stop on the beautiful Cayo Santa Maria. It was along this northern coast of Cuba that Hemingway set part of his novel ISLANDS IN THE STREAM, published posthumously in 1970.

OPPOSITE – A Siren Red 1954 Mercury Monterey Convertible identical to this, was the forty millionth car to come off Ford's production line in 1954.

The Chevrolets like this 1954 model, were the most popular American imports in Cuba.

OPPOSITE – A pristine 1954 Chevrolet Bel Air in the Parque José Martí in Cienfuegos.

A 1954 Chevrolet Station Wagon on Havana's Avenida del Puerto.

OPPOSITE – Powering down the Prado, Havana's grandest boulevard, is this 1954 Chevrolet decorated with a collection of non-standard hood ornaments.

A 1954 Chevrolet Suburban passes through the Plaza de Dolores in Santiago de Cuba.

OPPOSITE – 1954 Ford Customline.

A 1954 Buick Station Wagon in Santa Clara.

OPPOSITE – The Studebaker Commander Starliner maintained the brand's reputation as a style leader with its European influenced low sleek body shape created by Loewy designer Robert Bourke.

UP CLOSE AND PERSONAL

Somehow you find yourself stranded in a village east of Havana. There's a queue at the bus stop yet who knows when the next bus will arrive and where it will go. It looks as if it's about to rain and you don't have an umbrella. One of the locals suggests you flag down a car. A clapped out 1955 Dodge is chugging down the road. He stops and agrees to drive you to Havana. You sit in the front passenger seat which has no seat belt and you see bits of the road flashing past the holes in the cardboard below your feet. It's over 30 degrees and there's no air conditioning. Fortunately, the window is open and you use your hand to scoop in air. The driver powers up the old diesel engine to about sixty miles and hour, he turns up the music on the push button radio jerry-rigged to a USB stick and you thunder down the bumpy fairly empty road. The tropical rain starts to crash down and the driver fiddles with a switch but the windscreen wipers don't move. Unfazed by this, the driver continues to floor the accelerator. You need to wind up your window but there is no winder on your door. The driver notices, pulls the handle from his door and passes it to you. You manage to grind your window some of the way up before it jams open. It doesn't matter as you're pretty wet already, however you still slide closer to the middle of the expansive bench seat. Soon it stops raining. A little further down the road, at the next small town, he makes a left turn and stops to let you out. It seems that you obviously misunderstood about him taking you to Havana.

A 1954 Plymouth heads fifty kilometres out into the Atlantic Ocean, on the Cayo Santa Maria on Cuba's north coast. Here a series of narrow causeways and bridges leads to a string of pristine and stunning beaches including the Playa Perla Blanca.

OPPOSITE – A 1955 Chevrolet Bel Air without the Bel.

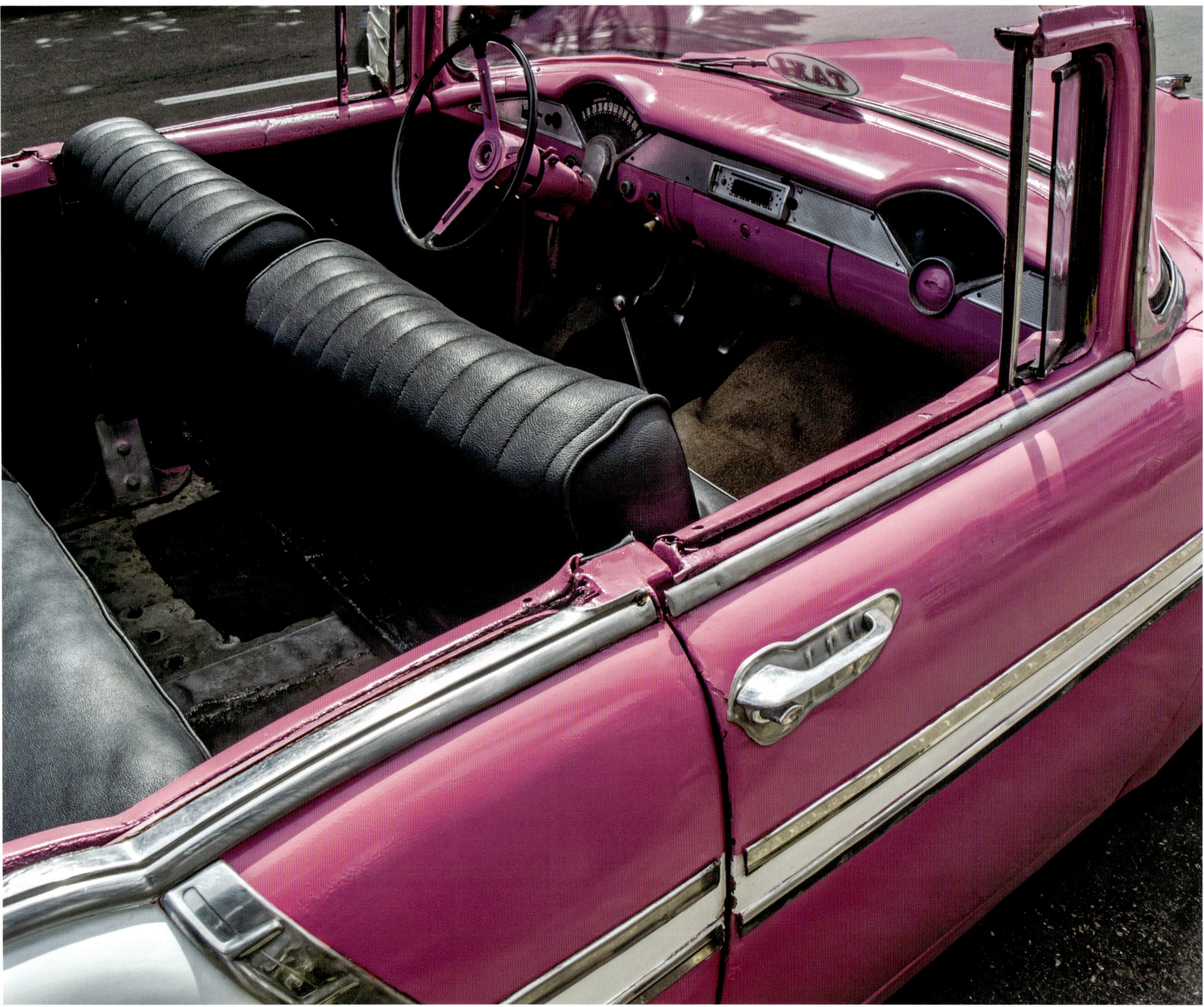

The extravagant fins of the 1959 Cadillac stand out from the pack. The 'continental kit', (the externally mounted spare tyre) is a popular facet on the dolled-up tourist cars of Cuba.

Opposite – All that glitters—the harsh reality of the interior of a 1956 Chevrolet Bel Air.

The flags of popular visitors decorate the rear vision mirror on a vehicle passing a 1958 Buick Super.

OPPOSITE – Cuban ingenuity displayed on this funkily crafted dashboard.

A Havana taxi heads down San Lazaro towards the 1950s Hotel Deauville which still boasts a 'swim in the sky' rooftop pool.

OPPOSITE – Inside the 1957 Plymouth Fury.

GRANMA, Cuba's state controlled newspaper, makes a handy mask for this on street spray job.

OPPOSITE – Happy snap.

The fin of a 1957 Chevrolet Bel Air with fuel filler cap concealed in the left hand fin trim.

OPPOSITE – Perhaps the most elegant and collectible of the cars of the 1950s is the 1957 Chevrolet Bel Air. Taking a leaf out of the Buick style book are the Ventiports next to the head-lamp.

The fin of a 1957 Chevrolet Bel Air

OPPOSITE LEFT – 1957 Chevrolet
Bel Air with over the top bomb sight
hood ornament.

OPPOSITE RIGHT – The 1955
Chevrolet Bel Air hood ornament.

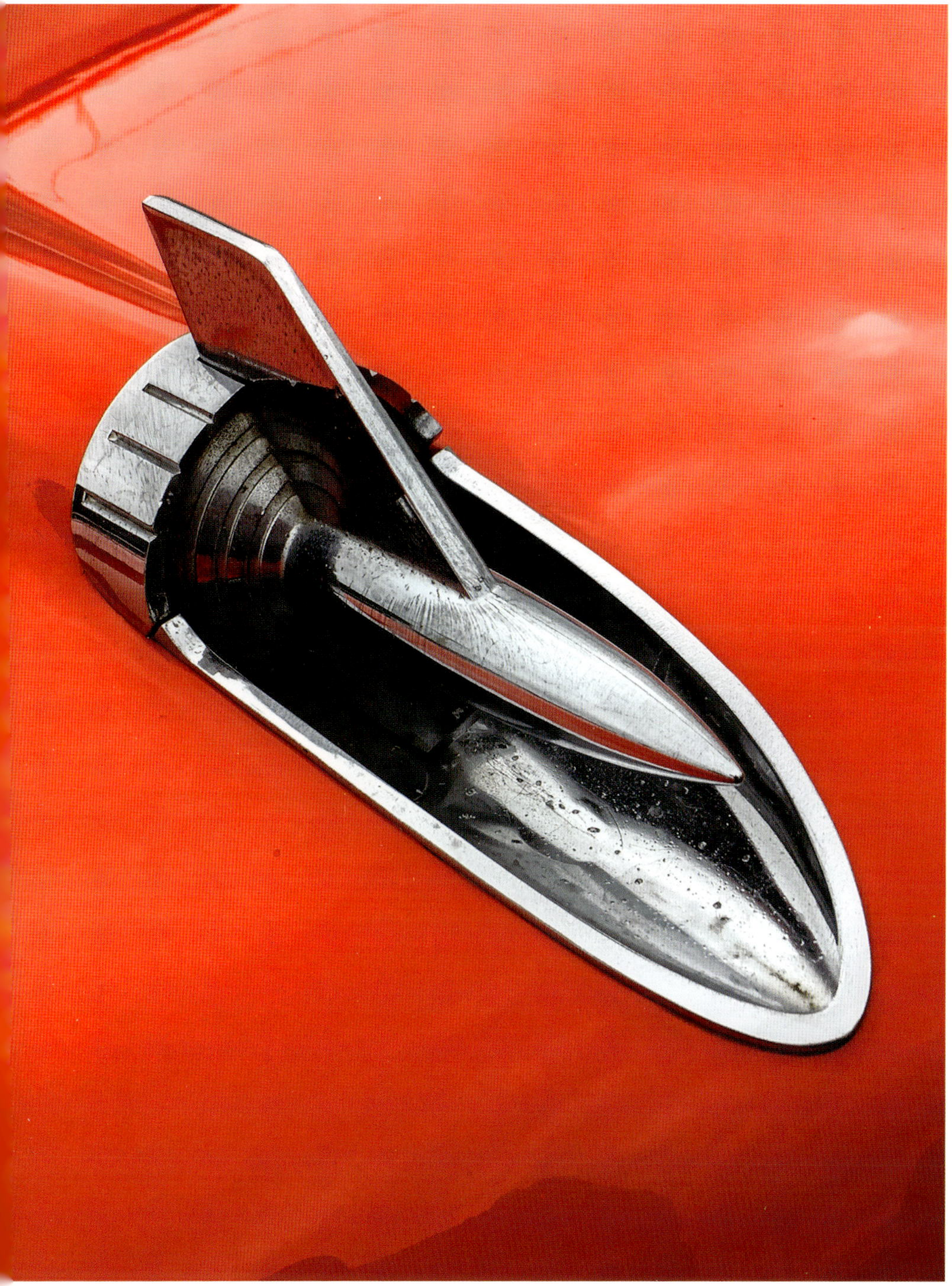

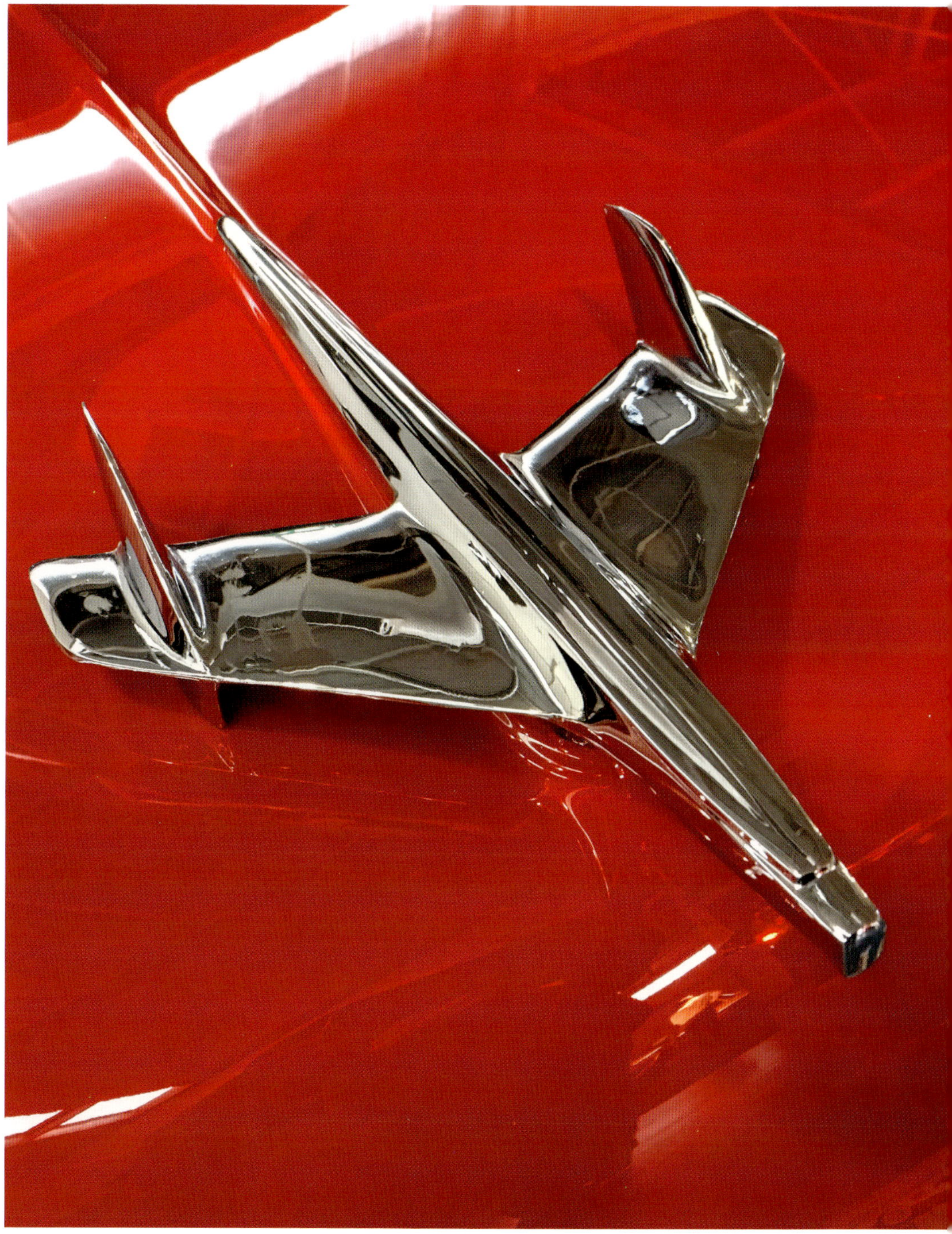

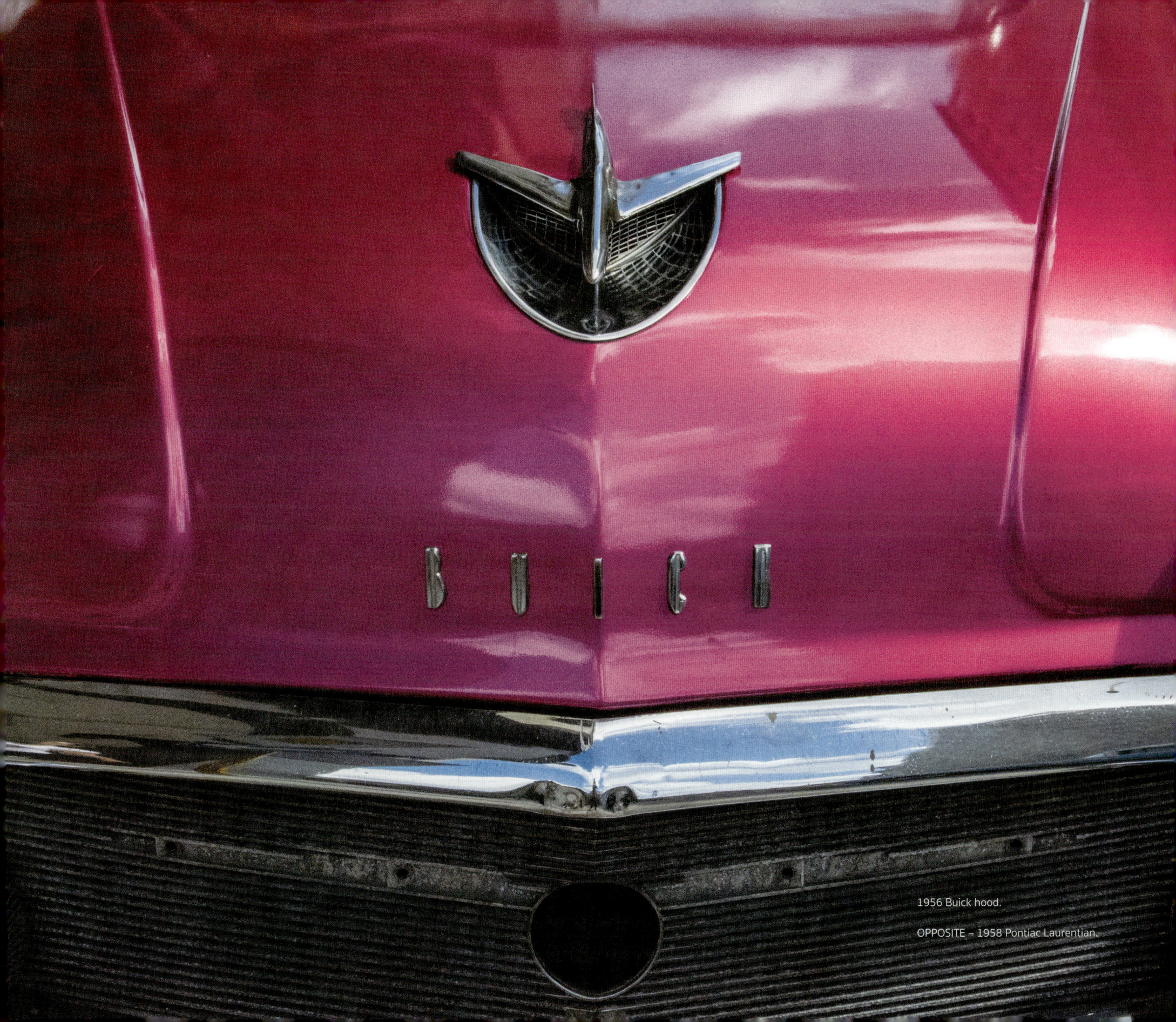

1956 Buick hood.

OPPOSITE – 1958 Pontiac Laurentian.

ABOVE LEFT – 1956 Ford Fairlane.

ABOVE RIGHT – 1956 Ford Fairlane Rear Badge.

OPPOSITE – The tail of a 1954 Buick Eight.

1957 Ford Fairlane.

OPPOSITE – 1957 Custom 300 Fordor.

Hood ornament or hoodoo ornament?

OPPOSITE – 1952 Cadillac Fleetwood.

FABULOUS FINS AND FIDEL 1955–1959

1955, what a year! Disneyland opened its doors, the Mickey Mouse Club debuted on television and the first McDonald's restaurant opened. Elvis, Bill Haley and Chuck Berry were being heard on the new pocket transistor radios. Rosa Parks, an African-American bus passenger, was arrested after refusing to give up her bus seat to a white passenger in Montgomery, Alabama and Ruth Ellis, the last woman in England to be executed, was hung at Holloway Prison. The Soviet Union signed the Warsaw Pact with its Eastern Bloc allies: Bulgaria, Albania, Hungary, East Germany, Poland, Czechoslovakia, and Romania. West Germany joined NATO and the USS Nautilus became the first operational nuclear powered submarine. Oh and Bill Gates and Steve Jobs were born and Albert Einstein died.

In Cuba, President Batista perhaps caught up in the zeitgeist and feeling secure in his control of the country, granted amnesty to all political prisoners. Fidel and Raúl Castro, only two years into their fifteen year gaol sentences, were freed and made haste to Mexico.

Havana in the late 1950s, became the place to be seen. Errol Flynn, Ava Gardner, Marlon Brando, Liberace, Marilyn Monroe and many others among the rich and famous came by plane and by boat. Celebrities were entertained at the Antilles answer to the Folies Bergère, the Tropicana, where they might see performances by international stars like Frank Sinatra and Nat King Cole or Cubans Celia Cruz and Beny Moré. They stayed at the Mafia controlled hotels including the Capri and the Riviera, gambled at the casinos spread around the city, danced the cha cha cha and mambo and drank mojitos and daiquiris.

Appropriately they would swan about in Cadillacs and Lincolns and the pantheon of other American vehicles that in this period would reach their zenith in size, power and most of all in their exuberant, extravagant styling. Tail lights and other adornments took their cues from fighter jets and space craft. Colours became two and three toned in bright pinks and aqua and yellow. Aluminium and chrome trimmings increased in length and width and became more decorative. Convertibles grew in popularity and sports car versions were introduced. It was the tail fins however, that had been developing modestly since 1948, which blossomed into massive wing-like appendages and came to define the longer, lower cars of this era.

On the 25th of November 1956, Fidel Castro would embark on the first leg of his campaign to liberate Cuba. With eighty comrades including his brother Raúl, Che Guevara and Camilo Cienfuegos, he set off from Mexico in a motor launch called the Granma. Five days later they landed in eastern Cuba. The mission was another debacle resulting in only the Castro brothers, Che and Cienfuegos and a handful of comrades to escape death or capture and make their way into the Sierra Maestra mountains. This was the inauspicious start to the Cuban Revolution.

In February 1958, the Formula One Grand Prix was being staged on Havana's scenic ocean hugging Malecón. One day before the race, World

Champion Driver Juan Fangio, from Argentina, was kidnapped from the Lincoln Hotel by members of Castro's 26th July Movement. The revolutionaries were successful in drawing international attention to their struggle and the Grand Prix went ahead without Fangio. There was speculation that the rebels also sabotaged the racetrack itself causing Cuban driver Armando Cifuentes to crash into the crowd killing nine people. The race was stopped and Stirling Moss who was leading at the time, was declared the winner. Fangio was soon released unharmed and declared his support for the rebels. The five time world champion, would return to Cuba later as a guest of Castro but would not win another world championship.

On New Year's Eve, December 1958, Cuba's dictator General Batista fled to Santo Domingo. Two days later, Fidel Castro made his inaugural speech to the people from a balcony in Santiago de Cuba, immediately throwing down the gauntlet to the United States saying: "This time it will not be like 1898, when the Americans came and made themselves masters of our country. This time, fortunately the revolution will truly come to power." It did not bode well for the future of the motor imports from Detroit.

With Castro in power, throughout 1959, the new government shut down or took over businesses, appropriated private property and nationalized industries and utilities. Thousands of Cubans departed the country leaving behind their homes and cars. In response to this billion dollar loss of American assets, President Eisenhower banned all exports to Cuba in October 1960. While new American cars were stopped, for a time, much needed spare parts continued to be shipped.

The Castro government imposed prohibitive taxes on any new motor vehicles with Fidel saying the country needs "tractors not Cadillacs." The numbers speak for themselves. In the last year before the revolution, 1958, over 7000 cars were imported into Cuba. In the following year, this was halved, and over the next twenty years a total of just 17,000 cars would come to Cuba. In 1958 there were 24 cars per 1000 in Cuba (while at the same time there were only 4 cars per 1000 in Japan, 6 in Spain and 29 in Italy) and the number in Cuba was the same thirty years later (while Japan had 251, Spain 278 and Italy 440).

1959, was according to journalist Fred Kaplan, "the year everything changed." This was the year the German Volkswagen Beetle was promoted in America with the slogan "Think Small." In the same year the British launched their influential and iconic Morris Mini and Detroit hit back with the compacts: the Chevrolet Corvair, Ford Falcon, Dodge Dart and Studebaker Lark. The times were a-changing.

It was thus a timely coincidence at the close of the decade. In America, the sixties would see the end to the golden age of the motor car and its fantastic fins, while Castro's Revolution put an end to its fabulous fifties and the last great era of motor cars in Cuba.

A 1955 Pontiac Star Chief with a 1951 Chevrolet and 1953 Oldsmobile.

It could be a product from the laboratory of Dr Frankenstein, this hybrid 1955 Buick zooming along a scenic road west of Viñales in Pinar del Rio Province.

OPPOSITE – A 1955 Ford Fairlane in Baracoa, passes the ubiquitous murals that constantly remind the population of the government's message, in this case referring to Fidel Castro, his brother Raúl, and the sympathetic President Chávez, who in the hard times of the 1990s, swapped Venezuelan oil for Cuban doctors.

This 1957 Plymouth Plaza is parked in Calle San Miguel outside the Arieto Studio responsible for recording most Cuban musicians since the 1960s on the famous Egrem label, including the Buena Vista Social Club.

OPPOSITE – The 1955 Oldsmobile Super 88 offered new features including a one piece windshield, turn signals, and a cigar lighter. As with the Chevrolet, Chryslers and the Studebaker of that year, the Super 88 would go on to achieve classic status in the years to come.

Parked in the street outside Havana's famous Hotel Nacional de Cuba is a 1955 Desoto Fireflite convertible. Designed with Virgil Exner's 'Forward Look', this model achieved sales success and also blew away its previously conservative image.

OPPOSITE – 1955 Plymouth Plaza.

1955 Chevrolet Bel Air Station Wagon.

OPPOSITE – This gorgeous two-tone 1955 Chevrolet Bel Air convertible illustrates the dramatic style transformation incorporated in this model especially when contrasted with the green 1952 Chevrolet beside it. The '55 Chevy along with the '56 and '56 models (the 'TriFives') is rated among the most attractive cars the company ever made. Hollywood admired its good looks too with the car appearing in movies like 'American Graffiti' and 'Two Lane Blacktop'.

This 1955 Pontiac Star Chief parked on Havana's Avenida Belgica, has seen better times.

OPPOSITE – 1955 Pontiac Star Chief.

An open-topped '48 Ford follows a 1955 Buick
Century. The sedan version of this Buick became
famous as Broderick Crawford's Highway Patrol car in
the hit TV series of the time.

OPPOSITE – A 1955 Ford Fairlane turns from Calle
Aguila onto Havana's Malecón.

A 1955 Chrysler Windsor on Havana's Avenida del Puerto. Ernest Hemingway drove a similar 1955 Chrysler, but his was the flashier New Yorker model. Before that, he drove a 1947 Buick Roadmaster.

OPPOSITE – Down in the boondocks of Regla, Havana with a 1955 Buick.

A 1956 Ford in Trinidad. This model
was the first Ford to feature seat belts.

An 1956 Oldsmobile 88 at a popular stop in Calle Neptuno where people try to get a ride. Catching a ride is known in local slang as *coger botella* (literally 'catch a bottle').

OPPOSITE – Ford's luxury marque, the 1956 Lincoln Premiere.

BOTH – 1956 Desoto Fireflite.

1956 Chevrolet Bel Air.

OPPOSITE – A 1956 Chevrolet Bel Air with the 1953 model across the road.

The gelato colours of the 1950s are entirely in keeping with the colours many Cubans favour for their clothing.

OPPOSITE – A 1956 Buick with the popular—and cheap—Ferrari logo affixed.

A 1956 Chevrolet is parked on the Autopista Nacional de Cuba, which is the main freeway traversing Cuba and runs 900 kilometres from the north-west to the south-east.

OPPOSITE – The classic tail of a 1956 Desoto Fireflite.

A 1956 Chevrolet Bel Air at the Plaza de San Francisco on the edge of Havana's old town.

OPPOSITE – A 1956 Chevrolet in the scenic Viñales area in western Cuba.

1956 Dodge Custom.

OPPOSITE – A 1956 Dodge Custom Royal Lancer passes Havana buildings that are in an even more distressed state than the cars.

1956 Studebaker President.

OPPOSITE – A 1957 Dodge Coronet in front of Havana's Museo de la Revolución, formerly the Presidential Palace. In the same year as this car—in an attempt to assassinate President Batista—the palace was attacked by members of the revolutionary FEU Movement. This action combined with a simultaneous attack on the national radio station resulted in forty deaths including leader and Castro ally, José Echeverria. He was driving a 1956 Ford Customline.

A 1957 Ford Fairlane born in the same year as Gloria Estefan—the Grammy award-winning songwriter and recording artist—who two years later would be forced to seek exile from Cuba with her parents, in the United States.

OPPOSITE - The majestic rear with relatively subdued flared fins of a 1957 Ford Fairlane on Havana's boulevard, the Paseo del Prado. James Bond drove this car in the Cuban scenes of the movie 'Die Another Day'.

A 1957 Ford Custom 300 Fordor with styling described as 'headlight eyebrows'.

OPPOSITE – The stunning 1957 Chevrolet Bel Air was immensely popular in Cuba. Its futuristic form was appropriate in a year that would see Sputnik 1, the first artificial Earth satellite, launched by the USSR on October 4th, 1957.

Only in Cuba would you see a 1957 Chevrolet Bel Air that looks this way and is still on the road.

OPPOSITE – 'tramps like us, baby were born to run' – Bruce Springsteen might have been describing this shabby 1957 Chevrolet Bel Air on the run-down edge of Havana.

1957 Dodge Custom Royal.

OPPOSITE – 1957 Dodge Coronet
and a 1954 Mercury.

The beautiful incongruity between the stunning 1957 Oldsmobile Super 88 Holiday hardtop sedan and the tumbledown Spanish colonial streets of Havana's Guanabacoa area.

OPPOSITE – 1957 Oldsmobile.

1957 Desoto Firesweep with
1952 Oldsmobile Deluxe 88.

P 036 650

The 1957 Plymouth Fury, launched in the US, with the slogan: 'WHO SAYS TOMORROW NEVER COMES? YOU'RE LOOKING AT IT! SUDDENLY IT'S 1960!'. One wonders how many Cubans would have wanted to suddenly leap forward into 1960, if they knew the consequences.

OPPOSITE – The 1957 Plymouth Fury could reputedly achieve speeds of over 125 miles per hour.

A 1954 Mercury convertible is taking tourists for a ride on the Malecón (*Avenida de Maceo*) which runs from the old harbour side of Havana five miles west to the newer area of Vedado.

OPPPOSITE – A Chevrolet Impala is parked next to the Havana cruise terminal, busy once more with tourists. The historic docking of the first American ship was in May 2016.

The 1958 Ford Fairlane with sporty styling influenced by the popular Ford Thunderbird.

OPPOSITE – 1958 Pontiac Laurentian.

In 1958, all the General Motors models showed off the new quad headlights. This 1958 Series 62 Cadillac also debuted with extra features like power door locks and signal seeking radio.

BOTH – 1958 Dodge Kingsway.

Stalking the old Chevrolet is a 1958 Plymouth Fury, the model that Stephen King endowed with supernatural powers in the horror novel and movie, 'Christine'.

1958 Chevrolet Impala.

OPPOSITE   Ford brought out their sporty
Thunderbird model in 1955, to compete with
Chevrolet's ground-breaking European inspired
Corvette sports car. The Chevys were soon out-sold by
Ford over the following years. With the increased size
of this 1959 model, which seated four people and had
the option of a massive 350 horsepower V8, the car
maintained its dominance.

THE MOST WANTED

CUBA P 124 372

The distinctive alien-bug tail-lights of the 1959
Chevrolet Impala upstage the demure rear of the
1956 Ford Fairlane.

OPPOSITE – The 1959 Chevrolet Impala, known as 'the
wild one', was the last but not least creation of GM
designer Harley Earl.

1959 Pontiac Parisienne.

OPPOSITE – A 1959 Chevrolet Impala travelling down Havana's Malecón. The next model, the 1960 Impala was one of the last US vehicles to land in Cuba after the revolution. A mint green version of this vehicle became Che Guevara's favourite car.

1959 Ford Fairlane 500.

1959 Buick in *Barrio Chino*.

OPPOSITE – The 1959 Edsel became Ford's legendary automotive folly costing the company over $250 million dollars and forever linking the name Edsel with failure. Today fewer than ten thousand Edsels survive and models in mint condition can sell in America for six figures.

1959 Studebaker Lark led the trend towards more compact sized cars. The model's launch revived the company's fortunes but couldn't prevent the demise of this historic marque four years later.

OPPOSITE – It's easy to see why tourists enjoy cruising the Malecón in open-topped American cars like this gold 1951 Chevrolet and the pink 1959 Cadillac Eldorado with its massive 45 inch fins that writer Walter McCall noted: 'they had reached ludicrous proportions and were of questionable taste'.

UN-AMERICAN ACTIVITIES

As you travel about in Cuba, you notice that the older cars are not just American but also French, Italian, Swedish and English. In most cases they are from the post-war austerity period when modesty and economy was the norm, so unfortunately, they don't possess the panache and grandeur of their American counterparts.

Historically, Cubans were importing European cars well before their love affair with the US brands began, with the Italians and French the first to make in-roads. By the heady days of the 1950s, in spite of the dominance of the larger, flasher models from Detroit, some foreign imports found a market. In 1957, however they only accounted for about 10 per cent of new car sales.

The 1960 embargo impacted radically on the flow of US cars to Cuba. No such restriction was applied to other foreign imports yet the vacuum was not filled. The Castro government deemed cars a 'luxury' commodity and imposed massive taxes on their purchase, so a $2,000 dollar Peugeot would end up costing $6,000. With the populace uniformly suffering from reduced incomes it was only a privileged few who could afford a car and so the expected proliferation of European imports did not occur on Cuba's streets.

A circa 1960 Opel Rekord from the West German company which was a subsidiary of the the US car giant, General Motors.

OPPOSITE – A Saab 93, parked in the UNESCO Heritage town of Trinidad. This Swedish car was known for its success in the 1950s motor rally circuit with champion driver Erik Carlsson.

A 1959 West German Opel Kapitan parked in the remote coastal town of Caibarién in Cuba's central province of Villa Clara.

OPPOSITE – An Opel Rekord P1 two-door sedan in Cienfuegos.

A West German VW Type 181 parked in front of a retro-styled apartment block in Havana's Vedado area. This vehicle was developed for the West German army but more were sold to the public from 1968 to 1983.

OPPOSITE – A 1950s Ford Prefect from England was the model that out sold VW in Cuba's small car market. It is parked outside Havana's famous and largest cigar factory, the Real Fábrica de Tabacos Partagás which was founded in 1845 and produces well known brands including Cohiba, Monte Cristo and Romeo y Julieta.

An English 1950s Austin A30 which is identical to the car my mother drove to carry out her nursing duties with the Silver Chain in Perth, Western Australia in the 1960s.

OPPOSITE – A late 1950s Zephyr from the English Ford subsidiary.

A 1970s Polski Fiat 126 looks at home in this colourful Cuban street.

FROM RUSSIA WITH LADA

When you stay in a *casa particular* (Cuban bed and breakfast) you tend to rely on your hosts for local information, as in where to change money, good food, music venues and inevitably to arrange transport to your next destination. You want a taxi to take you to the next town knowing most of the old cars don't have seat belts or air-conditioning and are invariably slow, so you specify as clearly as possible in your broken Spanish, that please, you want a newish car that has these features. Your host helpfully makes some phone calls and it's all arranged, a car such as you have requested will be there tomorrow morning at 8 o'clock. Ready with bags on the doorstop at seven fifty, there is no taxi at eight, or ten past or twenty past. Your host assures you that all is well. A half hour later they make some calls and re-assure you. Later still they inform you that they can't get the new car but they have found a friend with an older model. Oh well, you think, a 100 mile trip in a swift 1955 Buick or Chevy will go quick enough, there'll be plenty of room and think of the selfies with this old classic car. Finally you hope the car pulling up is not your car. But it is. Your taxi is a faded clunky 1960s Lada. There's no room for your luggage, no air-conditioning and no style. At least the lack of seat belts doesn't matter because you can't go faster than about 30 miles an hour.

The nationalisation of US assets in Cuba caused the expected dislocation of relations between the countries. Fidel Castro, ever the opportunist, saw the grafitti on the wall and declared himself a Marxist-Leninist. He snuggled up to the Russians, who were more than happy to have a satellite next door to their cold war foe the USA and so grew the marriage between Cuba and the USSR. Of course, famously the Russians deployed military forces on the island which culminated in the nuclear missile bases that became the thirteen days in October known as the Cuban Missile crisis. Without reference to Castro, Kennedy and Khrushchev sorted out a compromise and World War III was averted.

In spite of all that, the Cubans managed to hang onto to their big communist friend and they were granted favourable trading terms with their Comecon allies, especially cheap oil. In addition they were sold a range of Eastern Block vehicles, mostly cars, truck and tractors.

In a move that the car owners would in time come to regret, the government offered to swap their old American cars for new Russian ones. The result was that large numbers of classic cars left the country no doubt finding their way into the hands of collectors and the Cubans were left with boxy Fiat clones, the Ladas and Moskovitchs. At first these new cars were in better condition and cheaper to run than the big American V8s but the owners soon realised they were being duped. Forty years on, there's little doubt which cars the tourists prefer.

A Lada taxi in historic Trinidad. It's estimated there are over a hundred thousand of these vehicles in Cuba.

OPPOSITE – A truck from the Russian manufacturer VAZ, Volzhsky Avtomobilny Zavod. The company was also known for the Volga but better known for the Lada brand.

A Lada in Santiago de Cuba.

OPPOSITE – A Moskovitch (son of Moscow) in Santiago de Cuba.

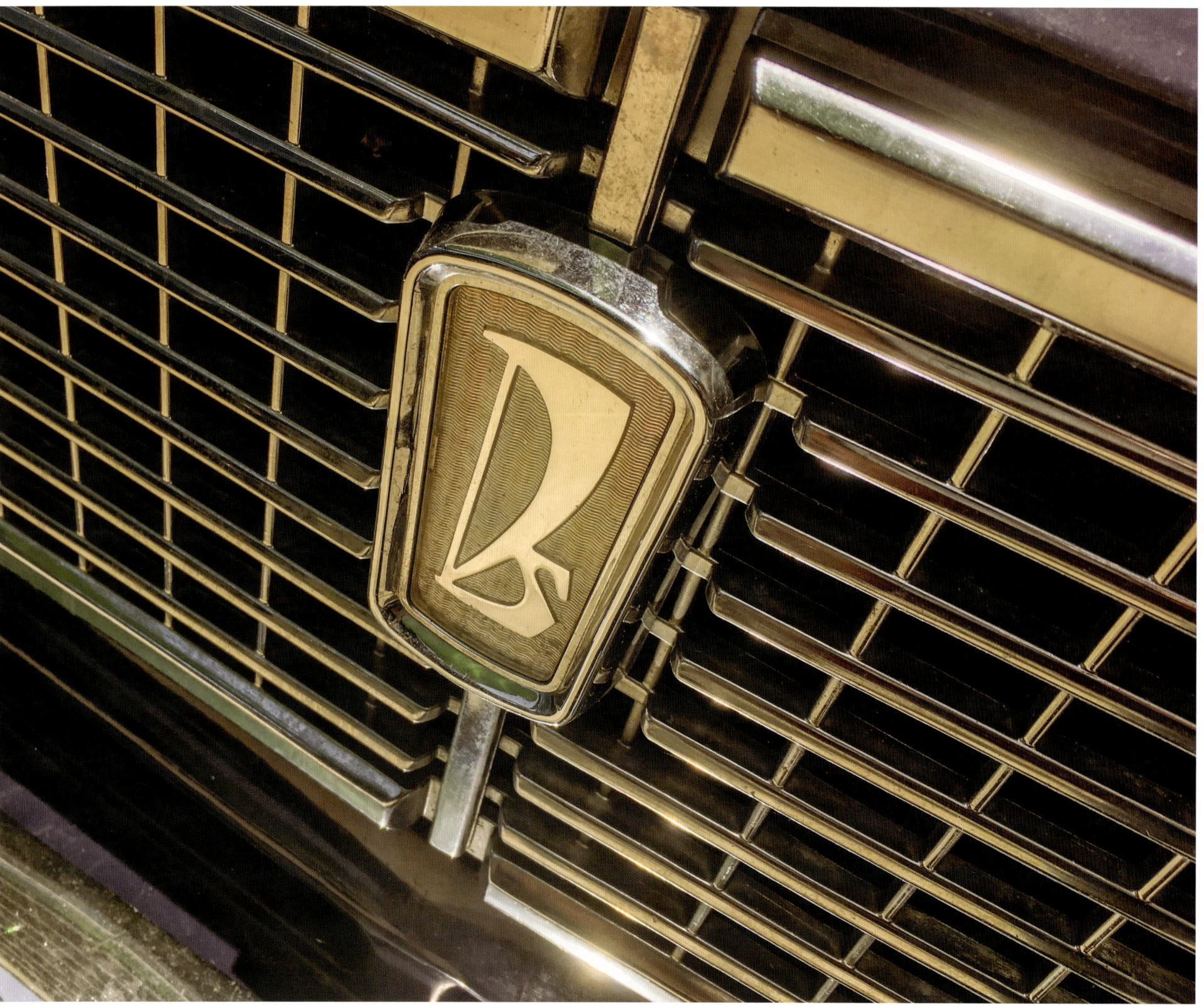

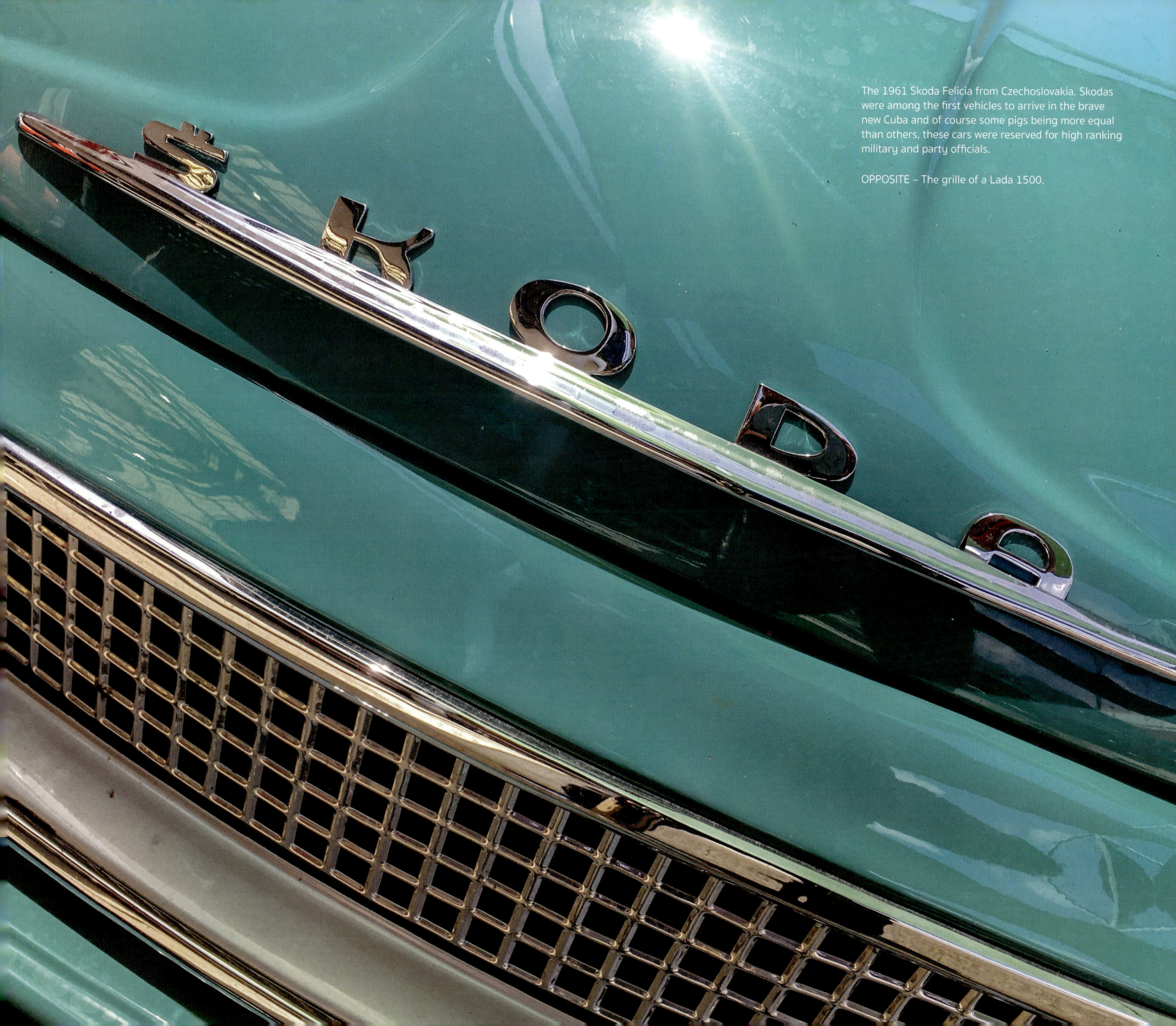

The 1961 Skoda Felicia from Czechoslovakia. Skodas were among the first vehicles to arrive in the brave new Cuba and of course some pigs being more equal than others, these cars were reserved for high ranking military and party officials.

OPPOSITE – The grille of a Lada 1500.

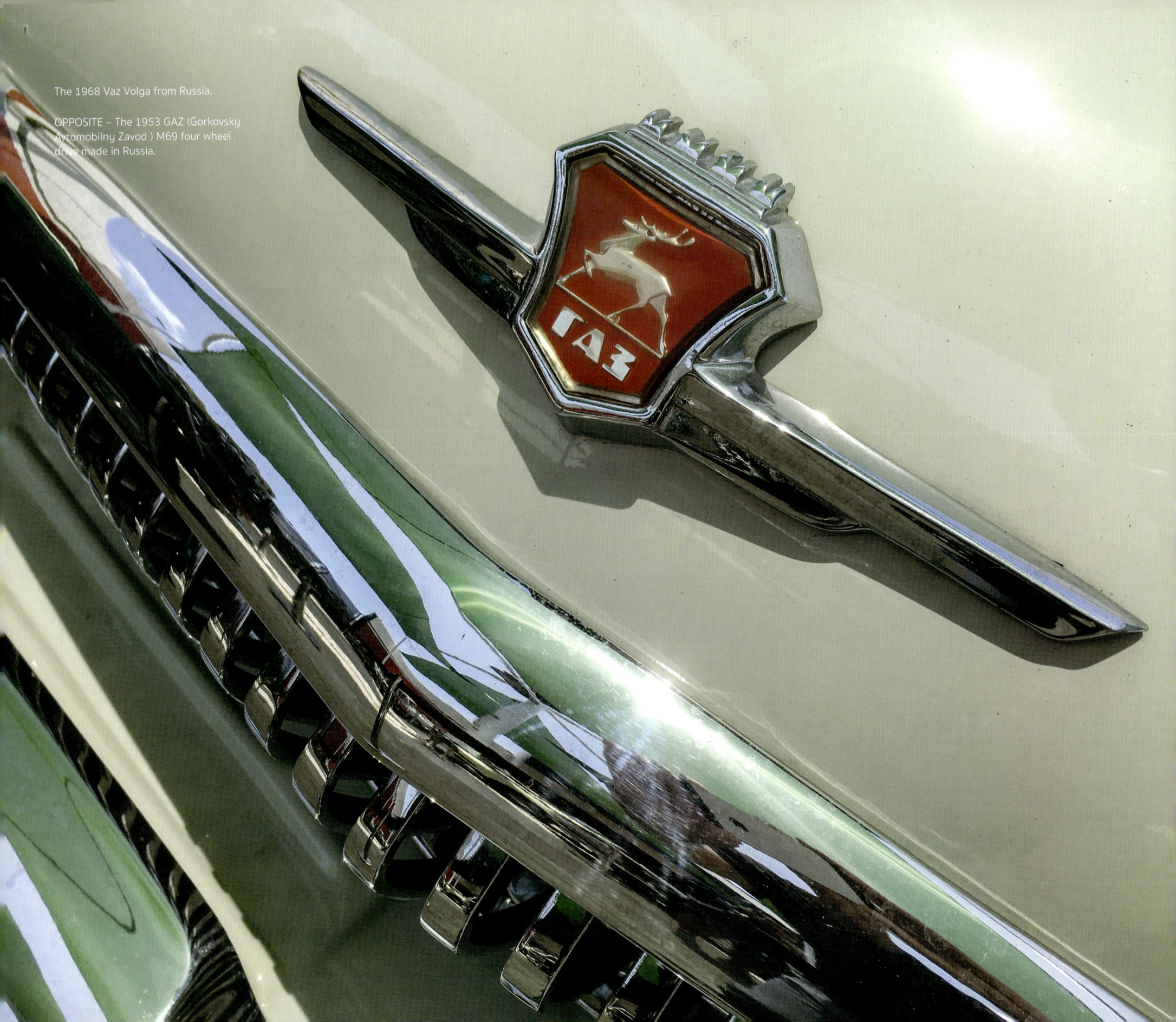

The 1968 Vaz Volga from Russia.

OPPOSITE – The 1953 GAZ (Gorkovsky Avtomobilny Zavod) M69 four wheel drive made in Russia.

A Gaz M69 four wheel drive light truck in San Cayetano in western Cuba. In 1971, it was replaced by the UAZ 469, the same vehicle seen towing the ashes of Fidel Castro across to his final resting place in Santiago de Cuba in 2016. On the last leg of his final victory lap, the UAZ broke down whilst passing the historic Moncado Barracks perhaps a symbolic reference to Castro's legacy of destruction perpetrated on this once prosperous island.

OPPOSITE – The Gaz Chaika, the Russian limousine. Soviet leader Nikita Khrushchev gave a similar car to Fidel Castro and it subsequently became the model used by officials in Cuba. These and the Russian Zil were known as *comandante*'s cars. Castro later received the gift of a Mercedes 560 SEL from Iraq's Saddam Hussein and henceforth the socialist leader retained the luxurious Mercedes brand as his car of choice, in particular the 600 series which was also a favourite of Nicolae Ceausescu, Pol Pot and Ferdinand Marcos.

This Lada in Santiago de Cuba is not going anywhere soon.

OPPOSITE – A well looked after 1960 Skoda Octavia (with fins) in Havana.

TROUBLE IN PARADISE

Travelling on the backroads of rural Cuba, you look across the fields and see a farmer ploughing his field with a pair of oxen. As if on cue, a man trots past on his horse, pauses, lights a cigar and canters on. A cart laden with sugarcane trundles along drawn by mules. A family make their way down the bumpy road in a carriage with steel wheels, pulled by a horse. You could be forgiven for thinking you've left the 1950s time warp experienced in the cities and gone back to the nineteenth century or earlier.

By 1991, the USSR had split into fifteen separate countries and all its eastern bloc satellites had turned away from communism. You might have thought Cuba would follow suit and move towards some similar kind of democratic and economic reforms but Fidel Castro proclaimed: 'Socialism or death' and so Cuba moved closer to death. Up until then Russia had bought Cuban sugar at artificially high prices and sold Cuba oil at reduced prices. Now the massive support and subsidisation of Cuba was over and the country was in dire straits with its economy shrinking by seventy-five per cent.

With no petrol and no money for spare parts, the country's cars, trucks, buses and tractors ground to a halt and roads were left empty. Cubans were forced to resort to other forms of transport. Mules and oxen replaced tractors, horses and bicycles replaced cars and man-powered bicitaxis replaced buses.

Twenty-five years later with no great advances or improvement of the economy most of these crisis measures created in what was known as the El Período Especial (Special Period in Time of Peace) regrettably continue on today.

Even two decades after the Special Period, alternative forms of transport are the norm as in a typical morning in Baracoa where there is a 1955 Chevrolet taxi, a truck, bicitaxis and several bicycles.

OPPOSITE — Cuban's answer to the rickshaw is the bicitaxi which came into being in the dark days of the 1990s when fuel was virtually non-existent. These humble conveyances were a way of providing oil-free transportation but they also became a means for people to become self-employed. Maintaining and repairing these simple machines remains difficult without access to spare parts, materials and proper tools.

Despite the high price of fuel and motor cars, there are fewer than expected motorcycles on the island.

OPPOSITE – A bicitaxi, converted for the transport of cartons of Havana Club rum passes a hybrid 1949 Plymouth taxi.

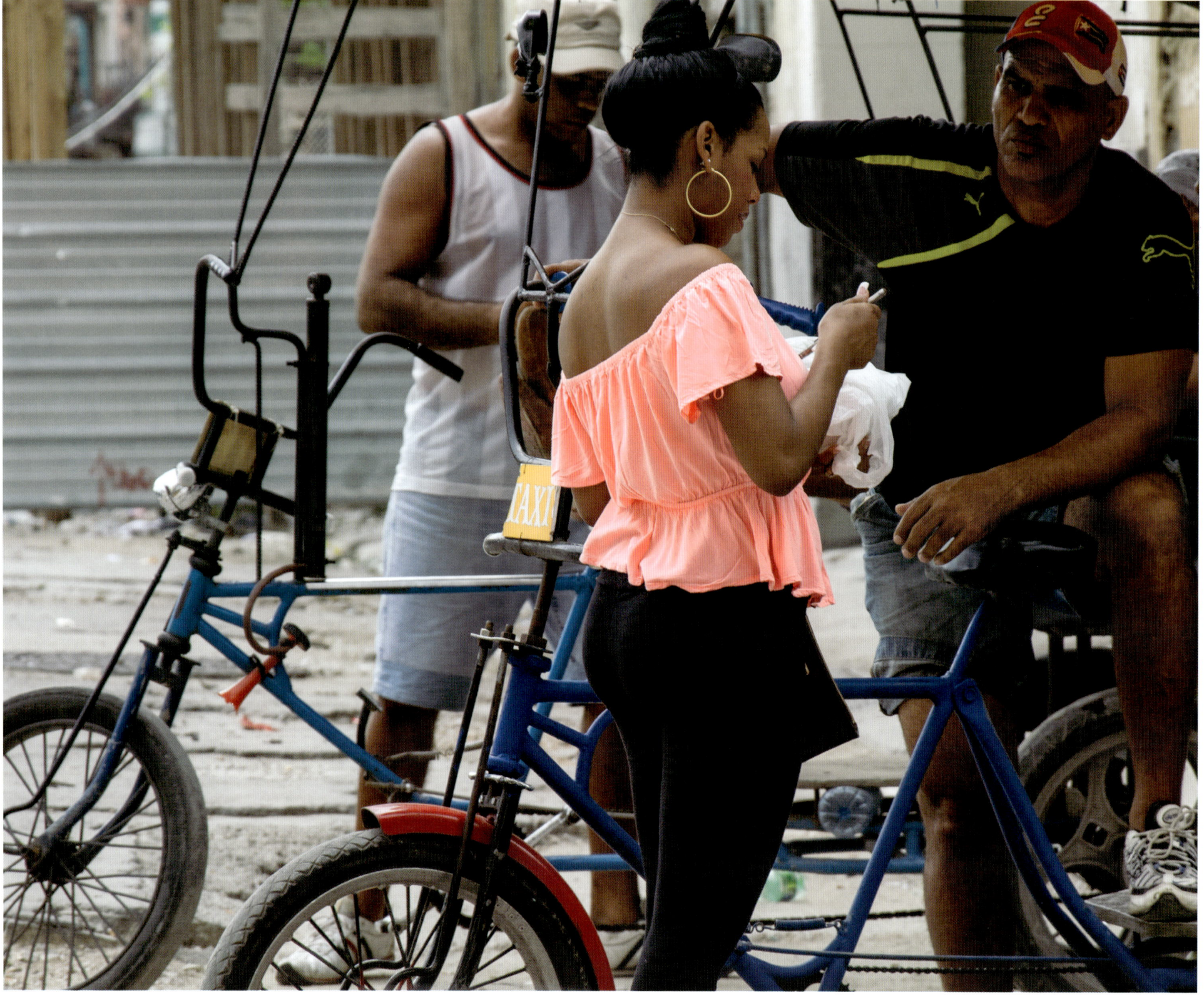

During the Special Period the Chinese government provided over one million bicycles which were sold to Cubans at a fraction of the cost. In addition, local factories were setup and these still produce 150,000 bicycles per year.

OPPOSITE – Bicitaxis are used by locals and tourists and are well suited to negotiating the narrow old streets of Habana Vieja.

The flat, traffic-free streets make
Havana an ideal city for cyclists.

OPPOSITE – The outskirts of Trinidad
where horses are the norm.

A *guajiro* (farmer) passes a tobacco plantation in Viñales.

OPPOSITE LEFT – Viñales farmer with oxen.

OPPOSITE RIGHT – Horsemen and cart in central Camilo Cienfuegos, east of Havana.

An ancient tractor belches and rumbles through Baracoa.

OPPOSITE – Horse drawn transport in Santa Clara.

Trying to catch a ride on the *camione*.

OPPOSITE – Travellers in Cuba shelter in the shade of a freeway overpass and wait for a ride. At some indeterminate time a *camione* (truck-bus) will come or they may get a ride with a *colectivo* (shared taxi). Hitching a ride is sanctioned and encouraged by the government and there are designated pick-up locations known as *punto amarillo*. These are named after the government officials wearing yellow jackets (amarillo is Spanish for yellow) who allocate the rides. Also government cars are required by law to pick up passengers if they have any spare seats.

OUT AND ABOUT IN CUBA

You're driving down a quiet typical backroad. As in Europe and the Americas, your car is left hand drive car and you travel on the right hand side of the road. Suddenly charging towards you, on your side of the road, is an old Plymouth sedan. Is the driver drunk or deranged or playing chicken as some kind of anti-imperialist revenge? You slow down, pull over and he swerves left and zooms past. This is not an isolated incident. As you venture further, after a while the penny drops. You realise there is nothing sinister in such an event and understand that the driver was simply selecting the best part of the decrepit road to drive on. Like the Cuban buildings and cars, the roads too are in an atrocious condition. It's bad enough driving along in rusty clunky seventy year old cars without the added drama of a road surface that is a nightmare of potholes and rubble. Worse still, after the rains, the pot holes fill with water and as you motor across the flooded streets you have no idea of the depth of pond you will encounter. Naturally in time you too will drive on the wrong side of the road to make your journey as smooth and safe as possible.

The Cuban roads are mercifully free from heavy or even medium traffic, which is fortunate as those who are lucky enough to possess cars want to drive them at speeds totally at odds with the state of the road surface (and the cars).

Whilst driving at night you will observe just a few major highways have any kind of lighting and find that darkness is the norm. What appears to be a solitary road is far from it and you will be faced with the prospect of encountering slow moving road users including dogs, cows, horses, vultures, horse-drawn carts, ancient trucks, tractors, pedestrians and cyclists. Railroad tracks also pass across the dark roads and there are no boom gates or lights to warn you.

Are there many accidents? The media in Cuba is controlled by the government, so as with the crime figures, the answer is anybody's guess.

LEFT – The wide open road, Cuba-style, delightfully free of traffic.

RIGHT – The turnoff on Cuba's main highway to the town of Australia, named after the once flourishing sugar mill there. It was from here (Central Australia), that Fidel Castro based his command centre whilst defending the country from the CIA assisted, Cuban exile attack in April 1961, known as the ill-fated Bay of Pigs Invasion.

LEFT – Highway signs in Cuba are used sparingly and once past the direction sign there are no additional signs at the actual turn-off indicating the right way.

RIGHT – Baitiquiri in the Guantánamo Province.

265

'GIVE WAY' or 'YIELD' sign in Trinidad.

Havana's petrol stations have not moved on from the 1950s and in a similar way to the cars, are in need of repair. Some Cubans bypass these pumps and siphon fuel from the tanks of state-owned buses and trucks.

ALL – Surviving 1950s style service stations in the
Vedado area of Havana.

CONSTRUCTORA PUERTO CÁRENA
AGRUP. 2
TALLER DE RESTAURACION
MARMOL - BRONCE - ALUMINIO Y
HERRERIA.

AREA DE
FUMAR
→

E
CIGARROS.

CUBA P 071 009

A workshop in Havana where Cuban
mechanics work their magic. Fuel guzzling
V8 engines may be replaced by old tractor
engines from Russia or newer diesels
from Toyota and other Japanese brands.
Bodywork may be spray painted but also
painting can be done with a brush or a
sponge. Bumpers and tailpipes are built
from scratch, piston rings cut from steel
pipe and pistons from a Volga may end up
in a Chevrolet. Even more basic maintenance
might involve using shampoo for brake fluid
and buffing using toothpaste.

OPPOSITE ~ The space left by a collapsed
building has become a grave yard for motor
vehicles. How many of these will be raised
from the dead in the years to come?

A beat up 1957 Chevrolet with its fins accessorised with the popular '55 Chrysler Imperial tail lamps known as 'sparrow-strainers', named after the device used to keep birds out of early jet-engines.

OPPOSITE – Green *maquina*, La Rampa.

A 1959 Chevrolet Impala at the Palacio de Matrimonios.

OPPOSITE LEFT – Once the Casino Espanol, now this elaborate building is known as the Palacio de los Matrimonios. It's the place where *habaneros* conduct their civil weddings. The decorated white 1956 Ford Fairlane will take them on a proud drive down the Prado and along the Malecón.

OPPOSITE RIGHT – The wedding party enjoy their traditional ceremonial cruise from the Palacio de Matrimonios.

THIS PAGE ABOVE LEFT – Calle Lamparilla in old Havana is a memorable locale in Graham Greene's 1958 novel 'Our Man in Havana'.

ABOVE – At the Easter fun fair, the kid's mini-car rides keep in character with their bigger on-road counter-parts.

LEFT – No translation required.

OPPOSITE PAGE – After the revolution, the communist government sought to cleanse the country of any reference to the Catholic Church and play down acknowledgement of the previous four hundred years as a Spanish and American colony. They therefore gave the streets more politically correct names replacing the saints with heroes of the Cuban wars of independence and revolution. The locals continue to use the original names causing confusion to out-of-town taxi drivers and self-driving visitors.

The top of the line 1957 Chrysler Imperial Crown was marketed as: 'Finest expression of the Forward Look'. It exemplified Chrysler designer Exner's dramatic rooflines and extreme tail fins which put the wind up rival manufacturer General Motors.

OPPOSITE – Drivers and their 1955 Pontiac Star Chief and 1957 Dodge Custom Royal.

THE ROAD AHEAD

Even with the removal of US sanctions and the increased detente, admirers and collectors of classic American cars will be hard pressed to get their hands on a Cuban example. It's highly improbable the government will change its stance on the sale and export of these cars particularly as they contribute so much to Cuba's allure for tourists and in spite of the ironic American connection, they are now seen as a national treasure.

In addition so many of the cars have been bastardised with different engines, handmade spare parts and odd wheels, they would require a lot of work and expense to raise up to standard. The need to conform to current emission and other safety requirements that are normal in countries outside Cuba, would also add to the costs. So even if they could ship the cars off-shore, cost-wise, most collectors and car-buffs would be better off seeking barn-finds in their own countries.

It's feasible that at some time in the future, spare parts will be allowed to be imported (many are already brought in un-officially by friends and relatives). Also mechanical and panel beating tools and equipment will become more available. These changes will result in the Cubans themselves renovating and restoring more if not all of their stock of these old vehicles over the coming years, no doubt fully aware of how lucrative these cars can be in bringing in the tourist dollars.

Technology may also come to the rescue with 3d digital printing making it possible to clone spare parts and accessories via the internet, circumventing the importation restrictions and costs and compensating for the fact that in most cases spare parts for cars of this vintage do not exist anyhow.

One day, the government may reduce the exorbitant taxes on new cars and one day the Cubans may earn a decent enough income to afford to buy a new car. Traffic signals, traffic jams and parking meters will proliferate and Cuba's empty roads will look the same as the crowded roads of any other country, full of look-a-like bland SUVs and sedans in shades of black and white. Inevitably the boxy Ladas and Vaz will make their peace with the scrap heap, nevertheless one hopes the magnificent Buicks, Cadillacs, Chevs, Desotos, Dodges, Fords, Pontiacs and Oldsmobiles will motor on as beautiful reminders of a time gone by and patches of brilliant metallic colour in the Cuban landscape.

And in the meantime, you can enjoy the sight, sound, smell and feel of these valiant relics which proudly bear their dents and scars from the hard years gone. And like Cuba and the Cuban people, regardless of the difficulties facing them, these resilient survivors just keep carrying on. Although, it's not easy, or as they say in Cuba: *No es fácil.*

ACKNOWLEDGEMENTS

I wish to thank my family, friends and colleagues who have contributed creative feedback, my wife for assistance with research, the Gosford Motor Museum, the Petersen Automotive Museum, the stoic people of Cuba for their hospitality and friendship and the awesome workers from Detroit, Michigan who made those great cars.

AUTHOR'S NOTE

Every effort has been made to provide accurate details and descriptions and acknowledge sources. I apologise in advance for any unintentional omissions or inaccuracies, any butchering of the Cuban-Spanish language and its phrases, places and names and in particular, the identification of vehicles. In my defence I must state, in relation to the cars, so many of them have been altered by their owners over the past decades, that reliable identification is difficult. I would therefore be pleased to insert appropriate acknowledgements or corrections in any subsequent published editions and readers are invited to contact the publisher or may contact the author directly by email to:
fugitiveidentity@aapt.net.au

BIBLIOGRAPHY

ABOUT CARS

1001 Cars to Dream of Driving before you die. London, Great Britain: Murdoch Books, 2012.

Backhouse, Fid, Fogarty, Kieran and Oliver, Sal. *501 Must-Drive Cars.* London, Great Britain: Bounty Books, 2009.

Buckley, Martin. *The Car: a book of classic motors. A celebration of the golden years of the automobile.* New York, NY: Anness Publishing Inc., 2001

Cotter, Tom and Warner, Bill. *Cuba's Car Culture Celebrating the Island's Automotive Love Affair.* Minneapolis, MN: Quarto Publishing Group USA Inc. 2016.

Darwin, Norm. *100 Years of GM in Australia.* Victoria, Australia: H@ND Publishing, 2002.

Georgano, Nick. *The American Automobile A Centenary 1893 - 1993.* New York, NY: Smithmark Publishers Inc., 1992.

Green, Rod. *Car The Evolution of the Automobile.* London, Great Britain: Andre Deutsch, 2012.

Gunnell, John A and Sieber, Mary L. *The Fabulous '50s The Cars, The Culture.* Krause Publications, 1992.

Heimann, Jim and Patton, Phil. *20th Century Classic Cars.* Cologne: Taschen 2015.

Mueller, Mike. *Ford 100 Years.* St. Paul, MN: Motorbooks International, 2003.

Olyslager Organisation. *American Cars of the 1940's.* London: Frederick Warne & Co Ltd, 1972.

Parissien, Steven. *The Life of the Automobile A New History of the Motor Car.*
London: Atlantic Books Ltd., 2013.

Parris, Michael. *Fords of the Fifties.* Tucson, Arizona: California Bill's Automotive Handbooks, 2000.

Sedgwick, Michael. *Cars of the Thirties and Forties.* London, Great Britain: Park Lane, 1990.

Sedgwick, Michael and Gillies, Mark. *A-Z of Cars 1945-1970.* Devon, Great Britain: Haymarket Publishing Ltd, 1986.

Smith, Jeffrey S., Collins, Charles O., and Pettit, Jennine. *Cacharros: The Persistence of Vintage Automobiles in Cuba* Focus on Geography, Spring 2013.

Wilson, Quentin. *Cool Cars.* London, Great Britain: Dorling Kindersley Limited, 2001.

ABOUT CUBA

Baker, Christopher P. *Cuba*. Washington, D.C: National Geographic Society, 2012.

Barclay, Juliet. *Havana: portrait of a city*. London: Cassel Villiers House, 1993.

Buddee, Kim. *Cuba's Evolution*. US: Schiffer, 2017.

Cameron, Sarah. *Insights Guide Cuba*. Insight, 2011.

Connolly, Sean. *Castro: a beginners' guide*. London: Hodder & Stoughton Educational, 2002.

Cooke, Julia. *The other side of paradise*. US: Avalon Publishing Group, 2014.

Corbett, Ben. *This is Cuba: an outlaw culture survives*. Basic Books, 2004.

Eckert, Amy. S, Fox, Esme, MacKinnon, Dorothy and Van Fleet, Jeffery. *Cuba*. New York, NY: Fodor's, 2016

Gott, Richard. *Cuba: a new history*. Yale University Press, 2004.

Greene, Graham. *Our man in Havana*. London, UK: Vintage, 2004.

Hatchwell, Emily and Simon Calder. *Cuba in Focus*. London: Latin America Bureau (Research and Action) Ltd., 1995.

Hatchwell, Emily and Simon Calder. *Cuba: a guide to the people, politics and culture*. Interlink Pub Group Inc., USA: 1998.

Millar, Peter. *Slow train to Guantanamo*. UK: Arcadia Books, 2013.

Moruzzi, Peter. *Havana before Castro: when Cuba was a tropical playground*. Gibbs Smith, 2008.

Suchlicki, Jaime. *Cuba: From Columbus to Castro and beyond*. Dulles, USA: Potomac Books Inc, 2002.

Sweig, Julia. *Cuba: what everyone needs to know*. New York, NY: Oxford University Press, Inc., 2009.

Timmerman, Jacobo. *Cuba: a journey*. New York, NY: Alfred A. Knopf,Inc., 1990.

DK Eyewitness Travel Cuba. London, UK: Dorling Kindersley Ltd, 2015.